Mark Cuban

The Way Life and Business Can Be Played,
Success Stories of a Brilliant Billionaire.

Jason Hamilton

The follow eBook is reproduced below with the goal of providing information that is as accurate and reliable as possible. Regardless, purchasing this eBook can be seen as consent to the fact that both the publisher and the author of this book are in no way experts on the topics discussed within and that any recommendations or suggestions that are made herein are for entertainment purposes only. Professionals should be consulted as needed prior to undertaking any of the action endorsed herein.

This declaration is deemed fair and valid by both the American Bar Association and the Committee of Publishers Association and is legally binding throughout the United States.

Furthermore, the transmission, duplication or reproduction of any of the following work including specific information will be considered an illegal act irrespective of if it is done electronically or in print. This extends to creating a secondary or tertiary copy of the work or a recorded copy and is only allowed with express written consent from the Publisher. All additional right reserved.

The information in the following pages is broadly considered to be a truthful and accurate account of facts and as such any inattention, use or misuse of the information in question by the reader will render any resulting actions solely under their purview. There are no scenarios in which the publisher or the original author of this work can be in any fashion deemed liable for any hardship or damages that may befall them after undertaking information described herein.

Additionally, the information in the following pages is intended only for informational purposes and should thus be thought of as universal. As befitting its nature, it is presented without assurance regarding its prolonged validity or interim quality. Trademarks that are mentioned are done without written consent and can in no way be considered an endorsement from the trademark holder.

Table of Contents

Introduction

Thank you for taking the time to download this book: Mark Cuban: The Way Life And Business Can Be Played.

This book covers the topic of Mark Cuban and his success, if you are interested in a man that has achieved big in his successes then this is the book for you!

Throughout it will teach you not only the skills that he believes young entrepreneurs should know, but how to begin your own business in the same way he has. This book goes into the depths of how Mark Cuban became the entrepreneur he is today and a great amount of knowledge can be learnt from reading into this informative Novella.

At the completion of this book you will have a good understanding of the skills necessary for becoming an entrepreneur. You just need an open mind and the time to read, to obtain a positive motivated frame of mind to grow your business.

Are you interested in what it takes to become a successful billionaire...?

Once again, thanks for downloading this book, I hope you find it to be helpful!

Chapter One: All About Mark Cuban

With the television success of his time, Mark Cuban has become synonymous in the business world as one of the elite players to not only take advice from, but to model in one's work. From his beginnings as a bartender at a place called Elan all the way up to his $3.2 billion net worth, it was no easy feat for one man to get there. He has jumped through many hoops, angered many bosses, and been through his share of sketchy/money-tight times to obtain the status he has now.

His first adult job was at Mellon Bank, in his hometown, after he graduated from college. But do not be fooled, his first true step into business was when he was 12 and went door-to-door selling garbage bags to pay for an expensive pair of shoes that he wanted.

Now, this was when banks were just switching over to computers, and it fascinated him so much that he began devouring whatever he could on the study of machines and networking. But, he did not want to stay in his hometown for long, so he left for Dallas and took a job with a company called Your Business Software. He was a sales person for this PC software company, and was teaching himself programming at the same time. His thirst for entrepreneurship was unquenchable, and his self-teaching nature was very inspiring to the people that first hired him. He was reading all the software manuals in order to sell their product better, which enabled him to learn the industry inside and out.

Even on the jobs that he did not care for, he always saw it as an opportunity to learn a new facet of what he was trying to conquer. In every job that he did not enjoy he saw himself as getting paid to learn. However, things did not pan out the way that he wished, and he was eventually fired from that position. But, there is always good that comes out of every failure, and that was the determining factor for him. That was when he decided to go into business for himself, and he eventually began a company called Micro-Solutions.

In this company that he started with, he was a consultant. He sold software from third parties, and then offered to train people on the software he was selling as well as configure their computers. In all of this, he was also taking that self-taught programming language and writing his own programs. He absolutely immersed himself in this world, devouring everything that he could about it, as well as practicing and reading up on all of it in his spare time. Eventually, he would find the foundation of his career with his company in hooking up businesses so that workers could share information between each other as well as reselling products that they would purchase and revamp. With just those two ideals, he grew the company from nothing to $30 million in revenue. He eventually sold it to CompuServe, and that enabled him to start all over again and start AudioNet. He acquired a partner, Todd Wagner, and renamed it to Broadcast.com.

The main idea behind this business was webcasting, which was essentially some of the beginnings of putting live sports events online for anyone to watch or listen to. He got the idea from wanting to watch and listen to his Indiana Hoosier games online, and he ended up taking the company from just the revenue he had all the way to over 300 employees and over $100 million a year! His billionaire success comes in when he finally sold this company to Yahoo for over $5 billion just before the "dot com crash." After all this happened with the crash, he decided he was going to diversify his wealth into an interesting portfolio so that he would not be hit hard if there was another one, and he played his cards right.

Todd Wagner, his partner in AudioNet, rode with him on another venture entitled 2929 Entertainment. This company provided integrated production and distribution of films and video. It should come as no complete shock that Cuban would eventually make the move to purchase Landmark Theatres. Alongside his theatre franchise, he also owned the film distributor Magnolia Pictures. And, as if he could not have his feet in enough endeavours, he is also the co-founder (along with Philip Gavin) of what is the first high-definition satellite television network.

Cuban also has his feet in many different start-ups outside from the ones he has acquired on his television show. He is an owner of a search engine called IceRocket, a partner in a peer-to-peer technology company called RedSwoosh, and is also an investor in Weblogs, Inc., which was later acquired by AOL.

With his ventures in the sports arena, he is the owner of the Dallas Mavericks. In 2000, he purchased a majority stake in the athletic team, and the team saw great success. In the decade that followed Cuban taking over, the Mavericks win rate went from 40% to 70%, with more wins than losses (which had not been seen in the 20 years before Mark Cuban bought the majority share). And, as the owner, he does not take a passive role, like watching from a skybox.

He is right there, in the thick of it, with a team jersey on and courtside seats cheering on his team. Which is beautiful, because that is exactly the way he conducts his businesses: right in the thick of it. Mark is also a bondholder of Zuffa, which is UFC's parent company, and has expressed much enthusiasm for beginning a mixed martial arts club that could possibly rival UFC in the future. He has also organized HDNet Fights, which is a mixed martial arts promotion that airs exclusively on the satellite television network that he helped launch. And those are just the successes. Believe it or not, he has just as many failed ventures underneath his belt as he does successful ones, and that is just as important to his business legacy as it is to having the successful ventures.

Whether you believe it was luck or planning on his part, there are undeniable traits, moves, knowledge, and passion that were behind every single venture he took on to get to that point. Whether it was a failure or a massive success, his drive never let him down, and he believed that he could get the job done and do it better than those that had hired and fired him in the past, and that passion and drive is part of what brought him to what he is today.

Mark Cuban has quotes that tackle the best tips he has for budding entrepreneurs, and this book will outline not only those tips he has for all entrepreneurs of all stages in their business building, but this book will also tackle how you can take steps in your own business just like he did to find the path you need to reach your fullest potential. And yes, that includes the potential that took Mark from where he was to where he currently is.

Chapter Two: Passion and Choice

"One thing we can all control is effort. Put in the time to become an expert in whatever you're doing. It will give you an advantage because most people don't do this."

One of the first things that marks the path to a great entrepreneur is the passion behind your project. Now, Mark does not necessarily believe in chasing your passion, especially if your passion is something unprofitable, or something that the market is saturated with. However, it is a good place to start. Have you identified what you love? What makes you tick? What fuels your desires and makes you get up in the morning? That is the very first thing you must identify.

Why? Because so much of starting your own business is sales. To get your product out there, you will need to sell it. To get your product into conventions, you will need to sell it. To land those orders that you want, you must sell it. Selling is the backbone to starting any business, and the more passion you have behind your business, the more likely it is that you can sell it. Your passion for your business makes you believe that your product is just as viable to be on the market as any other product.

We see Mark's passion in everything he does, and he recognizes that the only thing you can truly control in business, or in sports, is the effort that you decide to invest. When Mark was still working for the CEO that eventually fired him, he was devouring the safety and technical manuals for the product, reading up on the researches and studies behind the product he was selling, as well as teaching himself how to program! But his passion did not stop there, he also took that capital that he acquired from his first sale and went on to build other ventures in areas in which he saw problems.

His love and passion behind everything that he did drove him to, and through, every single venture (whether it was successful or not) that he ever decided to tackle. If your to do this for yourself the effort that you put into your business will not stop there. You must work hard to always find ways that improve your business. Mark has done this throughout his entire reign: from studying manuals and self-taught coding all the way to knowing the graces and downfalls of every stock he owns. Mark is always reading, teaching himself, and learning things to help aid him in his business endeavours and in his money. The effort you put into your business should be no different.

That passion also drives another major point in business: solving someone's problem. We hear Mark say it all the time in his television appearances: your business is not just a business, your business needs to have a purpose, and the best purpose to sell is the purpose of solving problems. If you already have an idea of what type of business you want to build, the next step is asking yourself if it solves a problem. Being able to identify with your customer their problem allows you to better and tailor your knowledge, your products, to better suit the needs of your industry.

People are more willing to purchase a product than a service, but the only service that outranks any product on the market is the service of "help." People will pay good money if the product you are selling to them is something that solves a problem they have. In one of Mark's start-ups, the problem was that workers in that business could not exchange information in a fast, reliable, and accurate fashion. So, he tailored his working integrity and his product to help them set up interoffice connections to trade information with just a few clicks of their mouse.

And he built a semi-empire on it.

How you may ask? Because being able to solve a problem in the industry you have chosen guarantees that you will have a unique product, and having a unique product is everything. If you want to continue repeating products and ideas of someone who has already preceded you, then that is like opening a franchise. You will not be able to build your own business around something as common as toothpaste. If you want to dream big and build a business that will be in it for the long haul, you must have something unique that you bring to the table. Just like Mark did.

Having passion for your livelihood is the backbone to any profession. Athletes would not train as much as they do if they did not breathe their sport. Teachers would not tolerate the kind of treatment they get from their government if they did not have a deep-seeded joy and love for dispersing knowledge. Musicians would not stomach the criticism, nit-picking, and negative outlook on their profession if they did not use it as nourishment every single day, and Mark Cuban would not be where he is today without the passion he has for his industry.

Having a business is the ultimate sport because there is always someone competing with you and trying to take your spot, and that is exactly how Mark views his business ventures: as a sport being played that needs to be won. One other thing that drives him through all of that is his desire. Having a passionate desire behind what you want to do with your budding company not only enables you to sell it, but it provides you with something to guide you through the hard times.

This desire to grow also assists you in ventures that fail. When Mark was fired by his CEO for insubordination (Mark Cuban picked up a $15,000 check that he was told not to pick up after making the sale), his passion got him through that tough time and even fed the spark that ignited the flare of entrepreneurship in him. Your passion is not going to just help you sell product, it is going to dig you out of the mine when you have fallen, yet again, and failed.

So, to recap: for you to begin your entrepreneurship with success, your product needs to 1) be a passion, 2) solve a problem, and 3) be flexible depending on your clients' needs. When you step in front of whomever you are selling to and make it all about you, it is ultimately going to fail. Once you grow your business to a point where you are selling your product to people who want to display you somewhere, it is no longer about you. You need to be flexible because flexibility keeps you open to possibilities you have not even come up with yet. People want a product or service that will help them so you need to ensure you bend and jump a few hoops to ensure customer satisfaction. By doing this it will not only make your customer happy with you but it will lead to further potential of business because the world is all about who you know sometimes.

Chapter Three: Solve The Problem

"Because if you're prepared and you know what it takes, it's not a risk. You just have to figure out how to get there. There is always a way to get there."

When solving a problem, one of the first questions you must ask yourself is: does my product provide the path of least resistance to something better? There are many people out there with awesome and wacky inventions but, in the end, some of them just end up making life more difficult. People might purchase that product for the novelty of it, or as a neat Dirty Santa gift, but no one will ever purchase it out of need. What you must convince people of is that there is a need for your product, and the way you will do that is by solving a problem that they are having with something that makes their life easier.

Look at what Mark did. When he walked into his first client's office when he was beginning Micro Solutions, his first customer was free. All he charged them was the cost of the software, and he trained the employees on it and set it up without charge. Even with Broadcast.com, once he got in there with his first customer, he realized that he could streamline a service that they needed and solve a problem that they had by sharing data between two desks with great accuracy and speed. He saw a problem, he solved their problem, and he did it without causing a great amount of headache.

Was it perfect in the beginning? Probably not, but this idea brings up another good point: potential customers love to see past customers, and that is a fact. Cuban offered his services free to his first customer and, in return, he got the ability to put his expertise into a growing business and show them as a past client to future clientele. Some clientele are just not willing to take the leap with a new business, and he found a very quick and easy way to navigate around that.

Sometimes the hardest thing to do is to pinpoint the path of least resistance between two goals, and that is where your business plan comes into the picture. If you are a new company sitting down and asking yourself, "how do I nail my first client?", it can be incredibly intimidating. Step back, and take a deep breath. Remind yourself of that passion burning deep within your gut and try again, and write out a business plan. Instead of asking yourself how you acquire your first customer, draw a bullet-pointed plan outlining each step.

For example: once you have an idea, you need a physical product. Alright, one step ahead. How do you get that physical product? First, draw out a model. Then, do your research and consult with someone who has knowledge of the production industry and ask them some questions, like whether your product is feasible in terms of production. They will be able to give you some sound advice on what is tailored for high-end production, what is better for mass production, and about how much it is going to cost you for that prototype. Then, you need to figure out what your margin needs to be.

From there, you can figure out the price of what you are selling, spend money for a few prototypes, and do a trial run. That trial run will not only give you a taste of what the market is doing, but it will give you working capital to expound upon. And, with that demo run comes feedback from the clients, which you can use to better your product. Then, once you have an item, a price, a test run, and some working capital, you can proceed on how to make your product better and how to pitch it to an audience.

This is a process that Mark talks about from time to time. In the classroom, when he was thinking about where he wanted to be in life, he decided that his trajectory in education needed to be based on what he wanted out of life. So, he started taking psychology classes to the University of Pittsburgh to help him read other people from afar. This might not be a business plan, but it sets the foundation of forethought, which is one of the skills you need to build and implement a business plan.

You yourself could also take this step as it is extremely helpful in understanding people and how to read different people. It would not only be interesting but it would develop your people skills in order to achieve better in your business ventures. All you need to do is get onto google and sign yourself up for a phycology business class in your area.

That talent of forethought helps him in every single meeting and negotiation that he does. Another example from Cuban: the points that he plotted to pay for his education. He set a goal, and that goal was to graduate from college. He recognized that he would have to find a way to pay for college, so he sought out ways in which that would happen. He began teaching dance lessons, and that morphed into him hosting massive, gaudy disco parties to which he charged admission.

When he transferred to Indiana University, he took that money he had scraped to save and purchased a bar in the area for $15,000. He used his business savvy that he had acquired along with his sales skills and he grew it into the most popular student bar around campus! He even started a chain letter that made him a little over $1,000. He had a goal, he broke down what needed to be done, and he set about ways to get there. And the thing was, it did not matter to him how many pots he had to juggle to get there.

If you have gotten this far, then you are on the right track. If you have 1) discovered your passion, 2) found a problem in it, and 3) figured out how to streamline that problem into a resolution, then you are further than most. The next thing? Cuban says it perfectly: "Get off your butt and do it." There are so many people in this world who have these grand ideas, but they never actually want to go obtain anything with them. Take the risk. Make the failures. As Cuban points out, "the failures might hurt, but you only have to be right once".

Chapter Four: Preparation And Your Company

"Wherever I see people doing something the way it's always been done, the way it's supposed to be done, following the same old trends, well, that's just a big red flag to me to go look somewhere else."

Once you have made the determination that you are going to take this venture on, that is when you should really start delving into Mark Cuban's story. There are some incredibly valuable lessons to be had from his experiences that can drive you exactly to where he is sitting now. One of those first lessons is to not ask anyone else to do something that you would not already do yourself.

What abiding by this idea does is it keeps you in check with your company and you in-tune with the people that you hire. If you have enlisted people to be on the ground floor of your start-up, and you have decided that the best way to approach this is to begin going door-to-door and selling to people, you better be able to do it yourself. When you are on the ground-level of a start-up, then that is the only level that currently exists. That means that you are on the same level as them, and they are on the same level as you.

If you expect them to go peddling your product door-to-door, you better be up the street with them doing the same thing. When you are beginning a business, there are no offices, and there is no privacy. There are no closed doors, and there is no managerial dynamic. There is nothing private in a start-up. Everyone is in the loop all the time, and not because everyone wants to be in everyone's personal business. But by having open offices and everyone on the same floor keeps the energy alive and everyone's spirits up.

You are starting this to build an empire, and you will pollute your business if you have a mind frame that you're the boss and no one is an equal, build your start up with a go get it frame of mind. You are here to solve a long-standing problem for years to come, and there is a difference in morale when you come at it from that angle. People enjoy working for other people when they feel they are appreciated and doing good. Your employees' morale is going to falter whenever there is a failure within the company, and trust me, you will have your failures. But an open office concept and keeping the energy up and morale high is going to benefit your employees during these times. When you take on employees, you are not just responsible for their job, you are responsible for their well-being while they are working for you. Make sure to always understand that.

When Mark bought the Dallas Mavericks, the first thing he recognized was that he needed to up the sales of tickets. So, he dragged every desk and chair out of offices, rounded them up on an open floor, moved phones over to every one of them, and sat with his employees as they proceeded to call every single ticket holder in the past year to get their advice, their ratings, and hear their opinions.

Mark was not about to ask someone he worked for to do something he was not willing to do himself, and that rule he keeps is in direct response to the CEO that fired him when he was younger. When that CEO fired him for picking up the check for his massive sale, he realized that his CEO was not willing to do what his employees do: he was not willing to continue to sell. His CEO believed that, since he had achieved his highest status, that he could stop working. Mark never wanted to implement that kind of strategy. He doesn't even consider himself the CEO of his own franchise, he calls himself the president! This idea is one of the reasons why Mark has become so successful.

But, this rule does not just keep you in check with your business, this also keeps you in-tune with whether those employees would be a right fit for your budding company. If you let them know that they will be going door-to-door, and one of your employees either does not agree with your decision or flat-out refuses to do it because "it's easier to call people" or "we can put up fliers", then you need to take a step back and make sure that this is someone that you want representing you and your business.

It is crucial, at the start of any business, that you have the right people representing you always. First impressions are everything. Mark constantly reinforces this when he talks about his former partner in many of his ventures, Todd Wagner. He knew where Wagner's priorities stood, he knew his outlook on blooming businesses, and Mark knew that he could trust him. Make sure that the people who believe in the same vision as you do are walking along the same path as you. This is one of the many contingencies that you need to be prepared for, which leads us into another tool for your belt that is going to incredibly important: preparation.

When Mark was in high school, he was already

preparing for things that could help him out even in the broad spectrum that he was thinking from in high school. He took psychology courses that ultimately enabled him to skip his senior year and enrol into college early. This not only saved him money, but it enabled him to pinpoint his focus even further. He knew exactly what he needed from his education to get where he wanted to be, and it all started with preparation in high school. Now, this does not mean that if you did not prepare in high school, that you are done for. It just means that, before you dive into anything, you need to take it bit by bit and make sure you prepare yourself for it the right way.

Preparation is something that will serve you well not only in the beginning stages, but throughout all the stages of life of your company. There are always going to be emotional risks. No one likes the feeling of failure. What this particular rule addresses is financial and business risk-taking. If you are educated, researched, and prepared, then nothing should blindside you in a meeting with a client. Not their company's overall earnings, not their company's net worth, not their company's growth. Nothing.

Being prepared, running the math, and doing your homework eliminates that risk for you. Know your industry inside and out. Know who your competitors are. Know their numbers and every product they have put out in the past two years.

Staying current on information will give you insight on how to improve, where your industry is heading, and give you a massive leg-up in product meetings with future clients. They will be impressed with your knowledge, and very fascinated with how you have researched their company and taken a vested interest in them. Otherwise, as Mark says, there will be someone like him to run you over in the meetings!

Product research is imperative, and preparation will aid you in that venture. It won't just serve you well when your company gets off the ground, it will serve you well before then, too. There is a lot of research, footwork, and crunching numbers that goes into building a product, so your knowledge base will start there.

You will need to know how your product is being made, what it is being made from, where you are making it, how many you can produce in a day, how much it costs you, and many other pieces of information that will serve you well when figuring out where to produce your product and how to distribute it among your buyers. Practice your preparation in the very beginning, and it will be a tool that is easily carried to other areas of your business.

Now that you have 1) found your passion, 2) found a problem, 3) fixed it with a streamlined process, and 4) made the determination to do something about it, we will discuss two of the biggest things that took Mark Cuban from where he was to where he is now, and one of them most certainly is not what you think.

Chapter Five: Effort

"Work like there is someone working 24 hours a day to take it all away from you."

A strong work ethic and the will to endure is the strongest, most valuable asset you can have as an entrepreneur. It will serve you well when you are using all your time that you can productively, even if it means you are only getting five hours of sleep at night and sleeping in a three-bedroom apartment with five other people like Mark had to in college.

A tip that he gives is to live as cheaply as you can so that you have more room for options in your future. At one point in time, Mark split a $750 rent six ways, stayed up until midnight so that he and his roommates could take advantage of the midnight grocery store chicken piece sale, and they would shield each other from cameras while they took turns emptying cans of Cheez Whiz into their mouths before putting the empty cans back on the shelf.

Even today, he still buys his soap, toothpaste, and razors in bulk! He crunches the numbers every year, and says that those non-perishable items that you can stash anywhere are worth purchasing in bulk. Most places that he buys in bulk at save him 50% in the long run, which amounts to about $1,000 over the course of that year. That is more than you would earn on an invested return on $10,000! Money that you earn throughout the year, except for a few instances, is usually taxed. However, money that you save for yourself by budgeting wherever you can is not doubly taxed. As Mark is always talking about, whether it is fully paying off your debt or buying bulk in underwear, "it is a guaranteed return on investment."

Now, this book is not suggesting you go out and squeeze Cheez Whiz into your mouth in the aisle of a supermarket, but the point is that he did everything around him in his power to save every single penny that he could so that, when the time came, he had the money necessary for an expenditure. Living well below your means (what most people consider cheaply) is less about what you are sacrificing and more about the opportunities you are providing for yourself. You do not need those luxury items right away to make yourself seem important. Remember, in every endeavour, you are not the important commodity, your product is.

At some point in time, every entrepreneur must grind out the long hours, forgo their personal comfort level, and dig their toes into the mud to get something done. It is just the nature of the beast. But, it is that nature that sets those that are passionate and believe in what they are fighting for apart from the those who are just trying to earn a cool buck with the next greatest thing. However, just because you put in the long hours does not mean you are being productive. Mark Cuban always tells his entrepreneurs that he has invested with to measure their success by the goals they set and achieve.

Measure your success by the amount of results you are seeing. A goal can be as simple as, "What do I need to do to deliver this to my client?" or as complex as, "How do I expand within my customers?" Time does not equal success. Achieving goals with your time equals success. Work smarter not harder!!!

Follow Mark's example: when he set out to create his own company after being fired, he had one goal in mind, and that goal was to be a better boss than his bosses. As far as goals are considered, that is about the broadest you can get. But, he still broke it down into workable aspects in his business plan, applied his strong will, and prepared himself for the haul ahead. The result? He has grown himself into the corporate man he is today.

The goals that you set for yourself are important, so you need to make sure that you not only set achievable goals with bullet-pointed plans, but that you allow yourself to dream. That dreaming and allowing your mind to think about what things could be like is sometimes the exact motivation you need when you get so frustrated that you throw your prototype down and walk away from the wreckage.

Mark did it. When he began Micro Solutions and was living in a three-bedroom apartment with five other guys, he would drive by all of the big houses and he would imagine what it would be like to live in one of them. Dreaming is not a bad thing, it is aspiring to that dream without a plan in place that gets aspiring entrepreneurs in trouble.

Even in Mark's dreaming, as his goals became loftier, he had a plan that he followed that was dependent upon the type of company he was building and that company's focus. As you can see, not all his companies focused on the same thing, but each focused on a singular aspect within the broad spectrum of the industry. It is because he researched, learned, and devoured all he could about the industry. Aspiring to a dream without researching the work involved, or having the knowledge of the industry and world surrounding it, gets people in trouble. Dream with practicality. Dream with a purpose. Do not let your dream be what tanks your business.

But remember, do not let this grinding it out and lack of sleep, or even a significant bump in the road, make you bitter. Part of the grinding it out, in Mark's story, are the failures of being under someone else's employ. Him being fired from job after job was gruelling and taxing on him, but he looks back on them now as models of what not to do when running a business. Some of the biggest lessons that will be learned in the industry you have chosen will come with your failures, and that is why everyone, including Mark, tells you to never be afraid of the idea of failure.

People who are afraid to fail fear the word "no", and in a world where you only need to be right once, it is preceded, and quickly followed, by a chorus of "no's". You cannot allow your fear to swallow you whole when taking on a venture such as entrepreneurship.

Even the toughest of venture capitalists become afraid from time to time. Maybe not about the same things that people just starting out are fearful of, but fear and nerves are there nonetheless. Do not ever fool yourself into thinking that success breeds confidence to a point where fear is innately conditioned out of someone. It does not happen. Just like the seasoned conductor of the New York Symphony takes deep breaths before going on stage, or that classically-trained actor wrings his hands before walking out to deliver his monologue, even the best in their field become nervous just before their big presentation.

Do not look down upon yourself for it. Accept it as a part of the journey and keep on going. Use your fear to fuel your thirst for learning. Know everything that you can before going into a "big performance." If you can eliminate as many unanswered questions as possible, you can learn to triumph over that fear that is innate within all of us, even though it will always exist.

The other big thing in Mark's arsenal that he has learned is that you need to always be nice to your potential clients. I know, sounds like an obvious trait, right? Contrary to popular belief, the amount of people Mark has encountered that begin swaying their hips in confidence, stand in front of a crowd, and try to convince them that they need the cocky person standing on stage is astounding.

This breed of people will stand up, rattle off all the reasons why they (instead of their product) would bring value to said company, and then expect to be treated with respect after disrespecting the same people who are supposed to be hearing them out as a client. Never walk in and think you are on a pedestal above them because of your product. They are not begging for you, you are there convincing them that they need your product. That process has absolutely nothing to do with you. Listen to their wants. Listen to their desires and long-term goals.

When a client feels that they have your undivided knowledge and attention, they are more likely to take what you are saying as expertise rather than opinion. Listen to what they say is broken. Listen to their problems. Become their friend that is there to help them find a solution, and then become their best friend that is going to tell them the solution to their issues. Do not act like a money mogul who is drooling over their check book. Make them happy with your solution. Solve their problems with a kind smile on your face. If you want to be the best, then you must provide the best, and that means the best customer service as well. As Mark says, "treat your customers like they own you, because they do." It is not their job to create their roadmap of success. It is your job to create that for them.

Knowing how to interface with customers is important. Not only do you need to know and understand how to sell, you need to know how to provide impeccable customer service. Mark did it all the time when he was working for his bosses, he did it all the time with every venture he began, and he even did it when he purchased the Dallas Mavericks!

He wanted to know why ticket sales were so down, so he sat at a desk with his employees and called people right along with them. If you thought you would be able to get away from interacting with people by creating your own business, you are wrong. If you thought you were going to be able to hire someone to do all of the personal interacting for you, you are wrong. When you first get this thing up and running, you are doing everything: you are talking to warehouses as your own branch manager and crunching numbers as your own accountant.

You are talking to unhappy customers as your customer service representative and taking feedback like a shift manager. You are setting up potential client meetings like the secretary and you are setting your own schedule as well as divvying up finances like human resources.

I know we have gone over many steps over the course of these chapters, so let's outline them briefly: from the very inception of something, you need to 1) find your passion, 2) find a problem within that passion, 3) solve that problem with your product, 4) decide to do something about it, and 5) prepare yourself for the long road ahead without losing your kindness. These steps are essential, and the realness that has been delved into with these chapters is something you must make yourself aware of and come to terms with. But there are things that budding entrepreneurs need to take away from Mark Cuban's story and they are that there are not all positives, and we will address these in the coming chapters.

Chapter Six: Stay Away From Investors

"Great companies start without investors."

In all that Mark has ever done, the one thing he never did do was take out a loan to start up any of his businesses. When he wanted to begin Micro Solutions, he pinched every penny he could save, continued to give his dance lessons and throw his disco parties, and sold his product and what he could offer door-to-door to potential businesses until one accepted.

He taught himself how to code so that he would not have to pay out-of-pocket for the code for his software, and he even offered his first client free training and installation if they purchased his product. None of this required a hefty, or even a small, loan from an institution. This is wonderful advice.

Seeing as Mark Cuban is a venture capitalist, and he is steering you away from all that venture-related money, I would suggest the advice be adhered to. Many starting companies feel as if they need to "appear important," so they will take out those loans and part of the money will not even be invested into the company. Instead, they take that money and purchase shirts with their logo on them, and then attempt to sell them to the public.

Mark has stated several times in his television appearances that never once has he attempted to sell clothing items to the public with his technology logos on them. Obviously, his sports team is different, but what Mark is attempting to get across is that the public is not going to pay $30 for a logo on a shirt that nobody recognizes, and it is a red flag for him that you do not understand how to spend your money well. Just like Mark never attempted to sell anything outside of where his industry lied, neither should you.

Instead, follow what Mark did: invest some time into a "side hustle." When Mark needed cash in college, he wasn't attempting to sell his programming software for pennies on the dollar, he was giving dance lessons! Everyone has an untapped resource...something they are good at but never had any passion to monetize. Mark gave those lessons and threw those parties for years while he was coding his own software, and it was only when he sold Micro Solutions that he had the working capital he really needed to do other things that he knew could benefit him. But, never once did he ever step foot into a bank to ask for money.

Another tip that he gives for blooming, or even thriving, businesses: credit cards are the worst investment. While he never stepped into a bank, he most certainly opened his own credit card. He has stated on numerous occasions that he wishes that someone would have instructed him on the money he would have saved and put back in his pocket had he not been spending it in credit card interest every month.

If you have the rolling income to pay it off every thirty days, then Mark suggests you do not run too fast to close it down, but he recommends that because of the experience he went through in his 20s to pay it off and close it down if you cannot pay it off every month. After all, if Mark can give dance lessons, throw parties, and scrounge enough to open a bar to provide revenue for future business ventures while working on his education, then you can find the time and energy just like he did to get the monetary assets you need. Remember the chapter where we discussed hitting the grind and working long hours? This is where that begins. And it pays off greatly, in the end.

Chapter Seven: Build Relationships

"I'm a believer that you can accomplish much, much more with direct relationships than by using an intermediary. And that cash you keep in the bank can be the difference between staying alive as a small business, or not."

His quote is directed towards PR firms, and this relates completely back to the sales skills that we addressed earlier. Those social interactions that you were hoping to get away from? They are going to do you a great deal of good.

You will take on those clients face-to-face, and you will begin to build trust. Build relationships. And, if you are lucky, you can build a strong enough relationship with the right person who will be more than willing to share their bigger contacts, which can open doors for even more interpersonal and inter-business relationships with people you would have never had access to otherwise. Mark's advice?

Those publications that you are reading to keep up with your industry have a publisher. Send that publisher an email. Introduce your company. As a publisher, it is their job to find new and amazing things to put in their publications on a weekly, or monthly, basis. A PR firm is not going to take that type of initiative. A PR firm is not going to be able to incite the kind of relationship and trust that is necessary for building bridges in business, which is why Mark never used them in any of his business ventures. Ever.

When it comes to stepping out into the world and making those relationships, Mark is not one to hold his tongue. From the tens of thousands of dollars, he has been fined by the NBA all the way down to the interjections on his television appearances.

Mark Cuban is a proponent of always making your voice be heard. It might get you into trouble, but if you are ready to apologize for anything said, then it is better to say it then risk the consequences if you do not. What he means is this: when you hold your tongue in the business world, you risk looking as if you are passive.

Passive, in the business world, can equal incompetence, and that is when you begin to quickly isolate yourself from the people in your industry that you could be building relationships with if you decide to put your best foot forward and cast aside the supposed idea of hurting someone's feelings or offending someone in the field.

Mark has always been a big proponent of speaking your mind, and what he states that he has learned in these many years in business is that, above all else, you have to believe in yourself. You must trust your gut and your ability to make decisions for your own business, and that you must take your own judgement as truth instead of using someone else's platform of judgement as truth.

Just look at his beginning: if he had allowed his family to have kept him in his hometown when they protested his going to Dallas, he would have never had open to him any of the steps he took to get to where he is currently.

In that situation, he was his business, and he trusted his gut judgement towards his life choices. Look at Micro Solutions: he went with his gut when telling his first customers that he would only charge them for the software, and it ended up snagging his first customer that drove him through the doors of many more customers, which ultimately built the empire that he had before he sold it off.

The best relationship, out of all the business relationships you will ever make, is the trusting relationship with yourself and your judgement of your own business.

Another thing that Mark warns businesses of: hedge-fund managers. He says that "the #1 job of a hedge-fund manager is not to make sure you can retire with a smile on your face -- it's for him to retire with a smile on his." Mark is a massive proponent of not allowing too many outside people deal within your finances.

Look at what he did: when he made his mark in the billion-dollar world by selling Broadcast.com, the first thing he did was he began to diversify where he put his revenue to have multiple sources of income. He made the decision not to drop every dime he had into the stock market, so he sold all his Yahoo stock; invested in Landmark Theatres, Magnolia Productions, the Dallas Mavericks, and a few other things to keep up a constant stream of revenue.

Then continued to work on other side projects to net him some sort of ancillary revenue. Diversify does not always mean the stock market. This information is important for growing businesses because it shows them that there are more ways to obtain revenue than just constantly investing your money into one thing.

When you are building your business, you should not be as concerned as this. However, when you get to a point where you feel you should have an outside source that you pay to manage your money, that is where these tactics that Mark utilized and learned on his journey come into play...and they are going to save you a lot of money in the end.

In this book, we have addressed many things to keep in mind when starting up a business. However, this chapter addressed some things you should stay away from when it comes to starting up, or growing, a business. The things you should stay away from are 1) loans, 2) credit card debt, 3) PR firms, and 4) any outside source, like a hedge-fund manager, who wants to charge you money to help you with your money. But, as we go into the wrap-up of this book, there is still one thing that Mark considers a massive proponent of success within any business.

Chapter Eight: Your Employees

"Keep a pulse level on the stress levels and accomplishments of your people and reward them."

Mark did it with his dance lessons and the parties he threw, he did it with the bar he purchased and opened, and he did it again when he purchased the Dallas Mavericks: keeping a check on your stress levels, as well as the stress levels of your employees, is going to benefit you greatly in the end.

Whether it is a massive vendor party or dinner or a long weekend vacation where you sit for four days in a hot tub, finding a way to alleviate your stresses, and the stress of your employees, is going to benefit you in the long haul. When Mark began Micro Solutions, he began doing a very special thing for his employees whenever they had a record sales month: he walked around the room and began to hand out $100 bills to every single employee.

At Broadcast.com, they had an alcoholic drink that was special to the company, and after a wonderful month all the employees would go out to a bar and indulge in this drink without a dime being spent from their pockets. This is not only a wonderful incentive to get your employees to work harder, but it is a reward for them once they do that ultimately boosts morale. That is one of the greatest things you can bring to your employees, and Mark did it every single month.

However, finding ways to relieve your stress levels

outside of your work and employees is just as important. Mark admits that he went almost eight years without a vacation, and he admits that he did not get the kinds of things accomplished that he could have had he allowed himself that break. Mark found it quite effective to start rewarding himself with special holidays every once in a while, it cleared his head space and allowed him to re think and become better focused.

As a new entrepreneur with a baby business, it can be hard to justify stepping away and taking time to yourself. You might be afraid that it looks unprofessional, or just outright lazy, but Mark has stated in several interviews that the reason he enjoys his pickup basketball games as much as he does is because he understands what it means to not give yourself that break. He understands the detriment it is on your body, your mental capacity, and your psychological withstanding.

Mark has admitted time and time again that there are always moments where he knows there is work to be done, but he never forgoes that pickup basketball game. He has scheduled that for himself, and he owes it to himself to take that time just for him. Take that time for yourself. It is imperative that you do, especially if you want to be responsible for uplifting your employee morale.

This time of de-stressing and gathering yourself will better prepare you for those moments that Mark insists will always come: the moments where you are kicked down or blindsided by something that you could not have accounted for. He says that you will never be judged by the fact that you are down, but that you will be judged for how quickly you get back up...and if you have not given yourself the kind of time you need to replenish your energy and your focus, you are going to overreact to a situation and do more damage than good.

It is always those little decisions that have the greatest impact on your business. You owe it to your business, in the long-run, to take care of yourself from the very beginning. Just remember, during those rough times that you are never going to always predict what hill happen.
Mark always tells himself this: "it's not whether the glass is half empty or half full, it's who's pouring the water." This helps him remind himself that, ultimately, he is responsible for his own happiness and the success of his company.

There are no shortcuts to this type of world. Mark worked hard and did whatever he could and whatever he needed to do to raise funds, teach himself his industry, create a product, garner that product credibility, and sell that product to businesses who would hear him out. His pedal was constantly on the floorboard whenever he was working and trying to make something of himself and the knowledge he was acquiring. Therefore, time to yourself is so important: without that rest and that time to "blow off steam", there is no way you can keep that energy level up to do what needs to be done to benefit your business and carry your employees with you.

Your business's health is directly related to yours, which is why you should never neglect yourself in the process of starting your own business. Mark understands the value of doing something you enjoy and makes you happy. It's the reason why he started HDNet, it was something he was passionate about and something he enjoyed. It is a lot easier to treat your business, and yourself, with respect when you are doing something that you enjoy.

Remember the entire passion point at the beginning of this book? This becomes relevant here, as well. However, this time it is all about respect: if you have respect for your passion, then you will do whatever it takes on your end to have the necessary energy to pour into it. That time you take might mean a long soak in a bath, or a couple of extra hours of sleep, or maybe even a massive week-long vacation. Whatever the case might be, if it helps you unwind, it will help you respect and be patient with your business as you continue to pour your energy into it.

Mark Cuban is a massive success story, and his story is filled to the brim with points and lessons that we can take away from it. If you are to emulate any trajectory of any corporate business mind, his would be it.

From giving dance lessons all the way to owning the Dallas Mavericks, the steps that he took...both good and bad...were imperative lessons that he took with him. Those lessons helped make him into the man he is today with the business acumen that he holds. From his self-taught coding days, all the way up to diversifying a $5 billion-dollar portfolio, Mark knows exactly what he is talking about, and his advice is so far out in left field that you can't help but think that he is onto something.

The tips in this book, both what to do and what to stay away from, will help and inspire entrepreneurs alike, whether you are just finding your passion or whether you are diversifying your own portfolio after your incredibly successful business.

Remember, making yourself stand out is going to be a massive goal when beginning any business. Talent does not make the business, the effort put into it does. Remember that effort chapter back up there? It applies here. Everyone believes they are talented, including Mark.

He will be the first to tell you that he is! He will also be the first to tell you that it is not just talent that gets you to where you want to be. If that was the case, we would have many more entrepreneurs than anything else in this world. It is the effort you put behind yourself to not just have great content, but to be unique and stand out, that gets you where you want to be.

The same applies to your business. Mark stands out in his field because he is one of the most educated. When he was beginning his businesses, he stood out because of other factors, like the employee morale boosters he was known for and the deals he would cut his first few clients just so he could secure them. He not only earned a reputation as a savvy businessman, he also earned a solid reputation as a good man, and that goes a long way with customer service and representation.

In the world of entrepreneurship, there are rules in place that help every single person wanting to start a business. If you can 1) find your passion, 2) solve a problem, 3) put in the effort, and 4) be flexible to what your clients need from you, then you are well on your way to beginning a wonderful, and trying journey. Make sure to take Mark's own story and use his lessons as your guideline, but do not forget the things he steered away from.

He advises you to stay away from 1) start-up loans, 2) credit card debt, 3) PR firms, and 4) anyone wanting to charge you money to handle your money. Stay away from investing in the stock market and use other ways of diversifying your monetary assets once you get to that point.

If you can follow these steps that Mark lived and learned in his own life and his own journey, then you have truly massive stepping stones on the right direction for whatever business you decide to delve into for your start-up company. Just make sure to keep one piece of wisdom in mind that has helped Mark time and time again: knowledge is power. Always know your market.

Conclusion

Thanks again for taking the time to download this book!

You should now have a good understanding of the steps necessary to determine how to start your business and can steer clear of all the fatal mistakes that new businesses make to get off the ground.

Now do as Mark Cuban did and get off your butt and work hard to achieve your business goals. But remember the key to succeeding is to ensure the time you spend is productive and you hit goals within set time frames.

The only person that can achieve your goals is you! I believe in you!

If you enjoyed this book, please take the time to leave me a review on Amazon. I appreciate your honest feedback, and it really helps me to continue producing high quality books.

Simply CLICK HERE to leave a review, or click on the link: (Insert link here).

www.ingramcontent.com/pod-product-compliance
Lightning Source LLC
Chambersburg PA
CBHW070719180526
45167CB00004B/1536